SPRING VALLEY

PLANET UNDER PRESSURE
POPULATION

Paul Mason

Heinemann Library
Chicago, Illinois

Editorial: Sarah Shannon and
Louise Galpine
Design: Lucy Owen and Bridge
Creative Services Ltd
Picture Research: Natalie Gray
and Sally Cole
Production: Chloe Bloom

Printed and bound in China by South China
Printing Company

10 09 08 07 06
10 9 8 7 6 5 4 3 2 1

**Library of Congress Cataloging-in-
Publication Data**
Mason, Paul, 1967-
  Population / Paul Mason.
     p. cm. -- (Planet under pressure)
  Includes bibliographical references and index.
  ISBN 1-4034-7741-8 (lib. bdg. : alk. paper)
  1. Population--Juvenile literature. 2.
Overpopulation--Juvenile literature. 3. Natural
resources--Juvenile literature. I. Title. II. Series.
  HB883.M37 2006
  304.6--dc22
                                      2005017063

Acknowledgments
The publishers would like to thank the
following for permission to reproduce copyright
material: Alamy pp. **20–21** (Iain Masterton);
Alamy/Eye 35.com pp. **40–41**; Alamy/
Photofusion pp. **34–35** (Liam Bailey); Corbis
pp. **20–21**; Corbis pp. **12–13** (H. Huey), **25**
(W. Cody), **34–35** (Liba Taylor); Corbis/
Bettmann pp.**10–11**; Corbis/Free Agents Ltd
pp. **29**; Digital Vision/Harcourt Education Ltd
pp. **26**; Impact Photos pp. **8–9** (Jerry Flynn);
Panos pp. **16–17, 28–29, 36–37** (Mark Henley),
16–17 (Jeremy Horner), **18–19** (Dieter
Telemans); Rex Features p. **22** (Colin Edwards);
Still Pictures pp. **36–37**; Still Pictures pp. **12–13**
(Mark Edwards), **27** (Steven Kazlowski), **38–39**
(Friedrich Stark); Topham/Image Works p. **32**;
Trip & Art Directors pp. **14–15** (Michael Good);
Trip/Viesti Collection pp. **6–7**; Trip pp. **4–5**
(Crasto Sherwin).

Cover photographs of high rise reproduced with
kind permission of Getty/PhotoDisc, and of
commuters reproduced with kind permission of
Magnum.

Every effort has been made to contact
copyright holders of any material
reproduced in this book. Any omissions
will be rectified in subsequent
printings if notice is given to the publishers.

The paper used to print this book comes
from sustainable resources.

Dedicated to the memory of Lucy Owen

Contents

Any words appearing in the text in bold, **like this**, are explained in the Glossary.

Population Issues Around the World

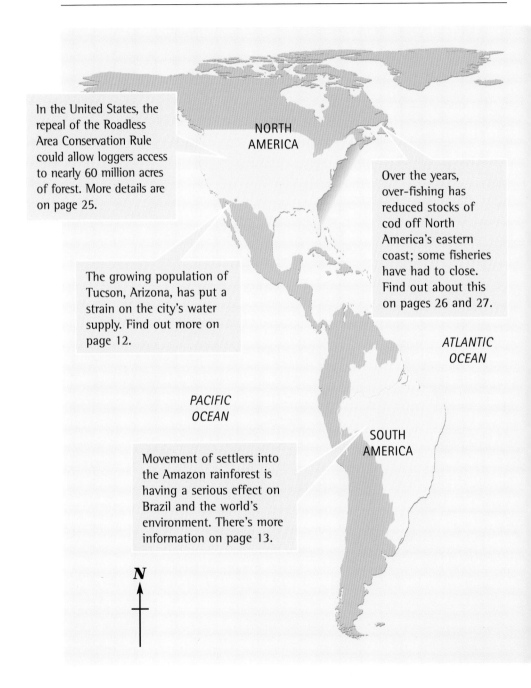

In the United States, the repeal of the Roadless Area Conservation Rule could allow loggers access to nearly 60 million acres of forest. More details are on page 25.

NORTH AMERICA

Over the years, over-fishing has reduced stocks of cod off North America's eastern coast; some fisheries have had to close. Find out about this on pages 26 and 27.

The growing population of Tucson, Arizona, has put a strain on the city's water supply. Find out more on page 12.

ATLANTIC OCEAN

PACIFIC OCEAN

SOUTH AMERICA

Movement of settlers into the Amazon rainforest is having a serious effect on Brazil and the world's environment. There's more information on page 13.

N

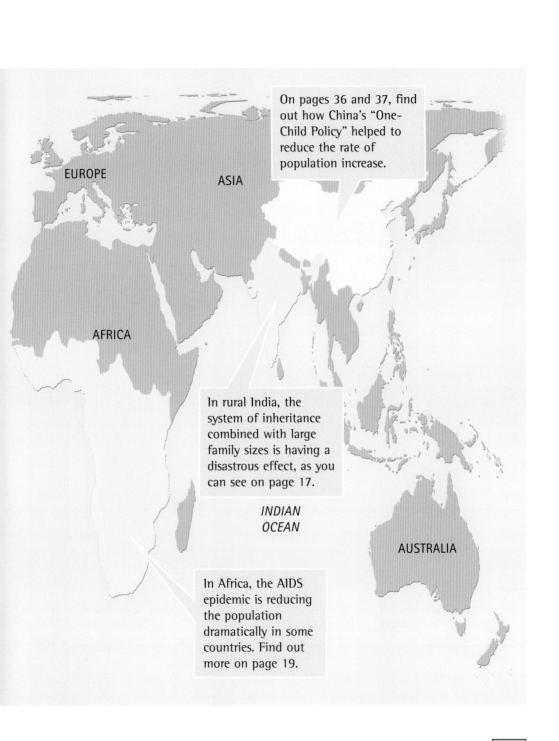

On pages 36 and 37, find out how China's "One-Child Policy" helped to reduce the rate of population increase.

EUROPE

ASIA

AFRICA

In rural India, the system of inheritance combined with large family sizes is having a disastrous effect, as you can see on page 17.

INDIAN OCEAN

AUSTRALIA

In Africa, the AIDS epidemic is reducing the population dramatically in some countries. Find out more on page 19.

A Crowded World

Our world is getting more and more crowded. In the year 2000, the world's population was estimated at a little over six billion people. This was more people than there have ever been on Earth before.

Estimates of the world's earlier population are what is called an "educated guess." We can try to determine how many people there were, but no one knows for sure. As time went by, though, governments began to count the numbers of people more accurately (usually so that they could collect taxes from them). Later figures for the world's population are more definite than earlier ones.

Growth in the world's population

How much has the world's population grown in the last 2,000 years or so? The **United Nations** estimates that in the year 1 C.E. there were 300 million people on Earth. By 1000 C.E., the figure was still only 310 million. By 1900, though, there were 1.7 billion people, and by 2000 our population had leapt to over 6 billion.

Put these figures another way: imagine the world as a bus that has seats for 80 people. The number of people in the bus represents the number of people in the world. In the year 1 c.e., there wasn't really anyone on the bus: the world's people occupied just 0.03 of a seat. By 1900, the bus was still over three-quarters empty: only 17 seats were taken. Just a hundred years later, in 2000, the bus was three-quarters full: over 60 seats were occupied.

There are still 20 or so seats on the bus, of course. But the world's population is still growing. Most estimates say that it is likely to be at nine billion by the year 2050.

Between 1950 and 2050 the numbers of people living in the world's four most populous countries will have increased dramatically.

1950			2050 (UN estimate)		
Rank	Country	Population	Rank	Country	Population
1st	China	555,000,000	1st	India	1,640,000,000
2nd	India	358,000,000	2nd	China	1,600,000,000
3rd	USA	152,000,000	3rd	Pakistan	381,000,000
4th	former USSR	103,000,000	4th	USA	349,000,000

Planning for the future

Growth in the world's population requires careful planning for the future. The increased numbers of people will need places to live, food, healthcare, education, clean water, and **pensions**, for example. Governments around the world must determine how they will provide these things for their citizens.

Life and death

The size of the world's population is dependent on birth rates and death rates. These are measures of how many people are born and how many die. The statistics of birth and death rates are one of the tools **demographers** use to predict future population increases and decreases.

Measuring population growth

Birth and death rates are often explained using a number per thousand people. For example, in 2003 Australia had a birth rate of 12.6 people born per 1,000 people. In the same year, 7.3 people died per 1,000 people (the death rate). Based only on its birth and death rates, Australia's population was growing by 5.3 people per 1,000, or 0.53 percent every year. This type of figure is not unusual for one of the world's wealthier countries.

In another example, in 2003 Panama had a birth rate of 20.8 and a death rate of 6.2. Its population was increasing by 14.6 people for every thousand, or 1.46 percent a year. This type of figure, or even a higher one, is not unusual in the world's poorer countries.

Alternative birth rates

Another way to predict population growth is by using a figure for how many children women typically have. On average, if a woman has two children, one will be a boy and the other a girl. So if all women have two children, they will add a man and a woman to the population, replacing themselves and the children's fathers when they die. In the long term, the population will stay the same. Because some children die before they reach adulthood, demographers usually say that women actually need to have an average of 2.1 children each for the population to stay the same.

Other factors in population change

Birth and death rates are not the only factors in predicting population change. For example, people sometimes move to a new country to live and work. Countries such as Bangladesh have a high birth rate, but many Bangladeshis leave the country to live elsewhere. This affects the overall size of Bangladesh's population.

Infant mortality

In the world's poorer countries, many more children die before they are one year old than in wealthy countries. The number of children who die before they are one is known as the **infant mortality** rate. It is usually measured by the number of deaths per thousand births.

- Infant mortality in richer countries, 2005: 5 deaths per 1,000 births.

- Infant mortality in poorer countries, 2005: 80 deaths per 1,000 births.

High infant mortality often leads people in poorer countries to have more children.

In 2005 the world's highest infant mortality figure was in Angola, where an estimated 187 of every 1,000 babies died before their first birthday.

Charting population change

Rapid changes in the size of a country's population are usually caused by a catastrophe, such as war or famine, or by mass **emigration**. More often, the populations of countries (and the world as a whole) change slowly, over time.

If the birth rate greatly increases in a country, it means many more babies have been born that year than usual. If this continues over five years, there will be many more children aged 1–5 years old than in the 6–10 age group. Five years later, these extra children will be aged 6–10. They will be going to school, so the government needs to plan extra classroom space for them. Leap forward another 60 years, and those same extra people will be **retiring**. They will probably need extra healthcare and other help.

Governments have to plan for the future. These babies were born in the 1940s. When they grew older, was there enough classroom space for them?

POPULATION PYRAMIDS

One way of charting population is through grouping people by age. In a classic "population pyramid," there are many people up to the age of 19 years old. This group is the wide "base" of the pyramid. After about 20 years old, sickness, accidental death, and other causes start to thin out the population. There are less people in the 20–29 year group. At this next level, the pyramid starts to narrow.

As people get older, increasing numbers of them die. At the top of the pyramid, the 60-years-and-over age group, there are relatively few people left. One example of a classic population pyramid comes from Nigeria in 2000 (see the diagram on page 11). Nigeria's chart is typical of many poorer countries.

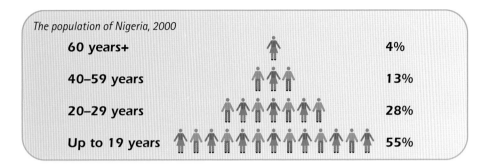

The population of Nigeria, 2000

60 years+		4%
40–59 years		13%
20–29 years		28%
Up to 19 years		55%

POPULATION MUSHROOMS

If people in a country start to have fewer children, begin to live longer, or if young people emigrate and leave the country in large numbers, the population chart begins to change its shape. Initially, it "bulges" in the middle. One example of this is the chart for the United Kingdom in 2000 (see the diagram below). This chart is like those of many wealthy countries.

The population of the United Kingdom, 2000

60 years+		20%
40–59 years		26%
20–29 years		29%
Up to 19 years		25%

If the birth rate stays low, or people begin to live even longer, the chart changes its shape again. Now it becomes more like a mushroom, with more people at the top than the bottom. The predicted chart for Russia in 2050 is an example of a population mushroom (see diagram).

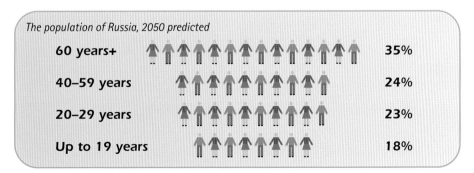

The population of Russia, 2050 predicted

60 years+		35%
40–59 years		24%
20–29 years		23%
Up to 19 years		18%

World Population Today

The world's population is still growing, but there are plenty of countries with large uninhabited areas. Australia, Canada, China, Argentina—each of these and others have vast areas with just a few people scattered across them. Surely there is plenty of room for more population expansion?

This is not necessarily the case. The land is usually empty for a good reason. For example, it may be a dry desert without water, or the land may be too mountainous. Another problem is that we need some unpopulated land. If the entire planet was settled, there would be no room for farmland. People would then find it difficult to get enough to eat.

When humans have tried to expand into new areas, it has not always been a complete success, as the case studies on these pages show.

Tucson's water

Since World War II, the city of Tucson, Arizona, has grown rapidly. Air conditioning, **irrigation**, and the use of **aquifers** for water have all made it possible for people to make their homes in the surrounding desert.

Tucson's growth is steadily draining the city's water supply. As the aquifer empties of water, there is a real danger of subsidence—land surface falling beneath buildings. The city is trying to conserve its water as much as possible, and hopes that new technology will offer alternative sources in the future.

The population of the desert city of Tucson, Arizona, grew from 45,000 in 1950 to 574,000 in 2004. This growth made tremendous demands on the city's limited water supplies.

Settlers in the rainforest

Brazil's cities have been growing rapidly since the 1940s. The government has tried a number of ways to slow the movement of people to the cities. For instance, people have been encouraged to move to sections of the country's **rainforest** instead. The government hoped the people could clear land there and make their living as farmers.

But settlement in the rainforest is controversial for a number of reasons:

- The settlers clear land without knowing which crops will grow best on it. Often the soil loses all its **nutrients** within a few years, leaving the land barren and worthless.
- Clearing the rainforest takes away the homes of local Amerindians.
- Settlers bring new diseases, such as influenza.
- Clearing forests also affects the animals and plants that live there, some of which are rare or endangered.
- The rainforest is an important part of our **environment**. It takes in and stores large amounts of rainwater and carbon dioxide. If this carbon dioxide were released into the atmosphere, scientists predict sea levels and temperatures could rise dramatically.

The rich-poor divide

The world's population is not growing at the same rate in all parts of the world. In some places, the population is actually shrinking.

Poorer countries

The rate of population change is closely tied to a country's wealth. The world's poorest countries usually have high birth rates. They also have high **infant mortality** rates and low **life expectancy**. For example, in Sierra Leone the infant mortality rate in 2001 was 316 deaths for every 1,000 live births. Life expectancy was 37.3 years. In such circumstances, people often have many children. They know that not all their children will survive. In fact, only 7 of every 10 children there will survive to adulthood.

Breaking out of poverty

If poorer countries become richer, they often develop better health care. More doctors and hospitals mean that more children survive into adulthood. People also begin to live longer. They continue to have larger families, but more family members stay alive.

LOWER INFANT MORTALITY LEADING TO POPULATION INCREASE

Imagine that in Sierra Leone, 9 out of 10 children lived to adulthood, instead of 7. These 2 extra people will grow up and in about 20 years will have children of their own. If the average family has 5 children, that's 10 extra children in 20 years. In another 20 years, 9 of those children will have had children of their own, making another 45 children.

	7 out of 10 children survive to adulthood	9 out of 10 children survive to adulthood
1st generation	♀♀♀♀♀♀♀	♀♀♀♀♀♀♀
2nd generation	♀♀♀♀♀♀♀♀♀♀♀	♀♀♀♀♀♀♀♀♀♀♀♀♀
3rd generation	♀♀♀♀♀♀♀♀♀♀♀♀♀♀♀♀♀	♀♀♀♀♀♀♀♀♀♀♀♀♀♀♀♀♀♀♀♀♀♀♀
4th generation	♀♀♀	♀♀♀

Population levels out

When countries reach a certain level of wealth, the speed at which their population increases tends to slow down. In Southeast Asia, for example, as the region has become wealthier the birth rate has fallen, from 5.3 births per woman in 1980 to 3.2 births per woman in 2001.

In some of the world's wealthiest countries, the birth rate has fallen below the level at which the population naturally stays the same size (2.1 births per woman). Immigration from elsewhere—often from poorer parts of the world—is one way for these countries to prevent the size of their population from falling.

The average number of births per woman in Southeast Asia has dropped from over five births per woman to just over three births per woman.

The world's poorer countries

In general, populations are increasing most rapidly in the world's poorest countries. Wealthy countries have much slower increases, and any increase is often due to **immigration** rather than high birth rates. Why do people in poorer parts of the world have more children?

PHYSICAL HELP AND INCOME

In some countries, people often have children so that they will be able to help with the family's work. This is especially true where many people make a living by farming. Even on a small piece of land, children can help with growing crops or caring for animals. The children grow to be strong adults and can take on more work as their parents become elderly and can take on less.

Countries where lots of people work on the land sometimes have high infant mortality rates. People tend to have more children, knowing that not all will survive to adulthood. If healthcare and living standards increase, more children survive.

Older children can provide help for their parents. Some move to cities in order to find work and then send money back home. In Latin America and the Caribbean, for example, poorer young people regularly leave home to work far away. They often send money home to help their families.

On small family farms in India, children are needed to help with the daily chores.

Land division in India

More than 50 percent of India's people make a living through agriculture (compared with 2 percent in the United States, for example). Most farmers practice **subsistence agriculture**, working on small pieces of land and managing only to feed themselves.

Roughly 25 percent of India's agricultural land is made up of large farms. The rest is broken up into tiny family plots. These pieces of land are continually being made even smaller. This is because when a man dies, his property is usually divided equally between his sons. A man with three acres of land and three sons therefore leaves them one acre each.

Over time, this **fragmentation** of land has disastrous effects, as it means some people own such small areas that they cannot grow enough food. Many must borrow money to survive. If they cannot repay the debt with interest, they often lose what little land they have.

Shrinking populations

In some of the world's poorer countries, population growth has slowed. Sometimes this is because a catastrophe has affected the population, or it may be caused by deliberate change.

CATASTROPHES

The size of a country's population can be dramatically affected by catastrophes, either natural disasters such as floods, or man-made events such as **civil wars**. Civil wars can have an even more terrible effect than natural disasters. After all, one of the goals in a war is to kill people from the other side. In countries such as Bosnia, Rwanda, Ethiopia, and Sierra Leone, recent civil wars have dramatically affected populations. In poorer countries, natural disasters can also affect thousands of people. When a terrible **tsunami** struck Southeast Asia in December 2004, the effects were disastrous. Hundreds of thousands of people died. **Cholera** and **malaria**, starvation, and a lack of clean water soon affected many more people.

In December 2004, a terrible tsunami struck Southeast Asia. In the aftermath, many people found all their possessions had been lost.

EPIDEMICS

When a disease affects many people more quickly than usual, it is known as an epidemic. Many diseases are spread by human contact. Epidemics affect crowded, overpopulated areas more often than anywhere else. Unless people have good healthcare and clean water available, diseases such as cholera and **tuberculosis** may spread quickly enough to become an epidemic.

Africa's AIDS epidemic

AIDS (Acquired Immune Deficiency Syndrome) is a blood-borne disease that leaves people unable to fight off sicknesses. It can be treated with drugs to prolong people's lives, but these drugs are expensive. AIDS has hit Africa the hardest. By 2003, nearly 20 million Africans had died of AIDS. More than twelve million children had been made orphans by the disease. Roughly 30 million people were believed to be infected with the HIV virus, which causes AIDS.

At a **summit** in Abuja, Nigeria in 2001, African rulers met and agreed to set goals to stop the spread of AIDS. AIDS is now considered to be an emergency. At Abuja, the rulers who attended the summit agreed to devote fifteen percent of their budgets to improving healthcare for their citizens.

The budgets of most African countries, though, are small compared to those of richer nations. Even with an increased percentage being spent on healthcare, many countries will still be spending only a tiny amount per person on the fight against AIDS.

CONTRACEPTION AND LITERACY

Contraception means taking deliberate action to prevent pregnancy. In some countries, men and women cannot find out about contraception because they cannot read. They may also be unable to afford contraceptives.

One effective way of stopping population growth in poorer countries is to increase the **literacy** rate. Once people are able to read for themselves about methods of contraception, they are better able to control the number of children they have.

The world's richer countries

Unlike poorer countries, the world's richest nations often have a very slow rate of population increase. In the United States, Australia, the United Kingdom, and New Zealand, for example, the population was growing by less than one percent a year in 2004. Some countries actually had decreasing populations, among them Spain, Germany, Italy, and Switzerland. What are the reasons for the lower population rates in these countries?

In richer countries, a much higher percentage of people commute to work every day.

WORKING LIFESTYLES

In developed countries, both men and women usually have jobs: many people want or need two incomes to afford the high cost of goods in richer countries. This makes it difficult to stay home with young children.

Children are not usually needed to help with physical work in richer countries. Nor are they crucial for help in old age like they may be in poorer countries. Instead, people pay into **pension** and social security plans that they hope will help support them as they grow older.

CHOICE

Increasing numbers of people in richer countries are simply deciding that they do not want to have children. Because contraception is available to anyone who wants it in these countries, relatively few people have children by accident.

Shrinking populations

In 2002, all but two of the countries with shrinking populations were in Europe:
Europe: Spain, Germany, Switzerland, Austria, Italy, Poland, Czech Republic, Moldova, Hungary, Serbia, Estonia, Latvia, Lithuania, Belarus, Ukraine, Romania, Yugoslavia, Bulgaria, Russia.
Asia: Georgia, Kazakhstan.

Fastest-growing populations

The countries with population increases of over three percent per year in 2002 were:
Africa: Sierra Leone, Liberia, Burkina-Faso, Niger, Chad, Congo, Democratic Republic of Congo, Djibouti, Somalia, Uganda, Burundi
Asia: Saudi Arabia, Yemen, Oman, Afghanistan
South Pacific Islands: East Timor, Solomon Islands

HEALTHCARE

Because healthcare standards are higher in richer countries, few children die while very young. In France, for example, 6 of every 1,000 children born die before their fifth birthday (figures from 2002). Compare this with Zambia, where the figure was 192 deaths per 1,000 births.

DEATH OF THE EXTENDED FAMILY

An extended family includes grandparents, aunts, uncles, cousins, and other relatives. In richer countries, people often live in small family units. People may no longer live near their families because they have moved away from home. This means the extended family does not live close enough to help care for children.

Extended families, like this one, now rarely live together in richer, developed countries.

Migration

Migration, the movement of people, can have a large effect on a country's population. Sometimes people within a country migrate from one area to another, but many migrants move internationally. People leaving a country are called emigrants; those arriving in a new country are called immigrants.

Many international migrants want to leave poorer countries in order to live in the world's wealthier countries. It is the wealthier countries that generally have the highest proportions of migrants. In the United States, Canada, the United Kingdom, and France, between 5 and 20 percent of the population was born outside the country's borders (this figure does not include refugees). Switzerland, Australia, and New Zealand have even higher proportions, at 20 to 49 percent. People who migrate solely for economic reasons are called economic migrants. Many undertake terrible journeys in the hope of building a better life somewhere else.

Other people migrate because they have been forced to leave their homes by war or **persecution**. These people are called refugees. Still others migrate simply because they like the idea of living in a different country—these are often people moving from one wealthy country to another.

The number of unaccompanied child refugees arriving in wealthy countries has steadily increased. These refugees have often escaped from areas of conflict and war. Many are frightened and find it difficult to communicate.

Migration figures, 2000

These figures exclude refugees, but show the difference between the numbers of people arriving and leaving each region of the world.

Region	Overall inward flow	Overall outward flow
North America	1.4 million	–
Latin America/Caribbean	–	0.5 million
Europe	0.8 million	–
Africa	–	0.5 million
Asia	1.3 million	–
South Pacific Islands	0.09 million	–

While wealthy countries attract immigrants, the world's poorest countries rarely do. In Nicaragua, Sierra Leone, Chad, Bangladesh, and Papua New Guinea, for example, less than one percent of the population was born outside the national borders.

ANTI-IMMIGRATION FEELINGS

Economic migrants and refugees often face a cold welcome waiting for them at their journey's end. Immigration is a touchy subject in many wealthy countries. Sometimes—particularly in Europe—people think that immigrants are coming to take advantage of the country's wealth, rather than to contribute to it. In fact, one way in which countries can add to their wealth is by allowing immigration from other parts of the world, thereby increasing the number of young people in their population who pay taxes. Despite this, immigration into most wealthy countries is strictly controlled.

THE BRAIN DRAIN

One problem for poorer countries is known as the brain drain. The brain drain is the emigration of the best-educated people in a country. Doctors and engineers often get permission to live in wealthy countries because their skills are highly valued. They can earn far more, and have a better lifestyle, than at home. But the brain drain leaves poorer countries without the very people they need to improve life for their citizens.

Impacts of Population Change

Sustainability

Sustainability is the idea that we should live in a way that will not hurt future generations. For example, if the slopes of mountains become **deforested** because people have chopped down all the trees, the soil is washed away. This means trees cannot grow on the slopes any more. Future generations will have lost a forest that cannot be replaced. Population increases can make it harder to live in a sustainable way.

FOSSIL FUELS

The use of fossil fuels—oil, gas, and coal—is one example of people acting in an unsustainable way. We use fossil fuels to run our cars, provide us with heat and light, and power our industries. In 2000, more than 80 percent of the energy we used came from non-renewable sources (meaning that once they have been used, they cannot be replaced). The bulk of this non-renewable energy came from fossil fuels.

Our high usage of fossil fuels means that we are slowly draining the world of its oil, natural gas, and coal supplies. This will also affect the world in the future. Burning fossil fuels releases **carbon dioxide** into the atmosphere. Fossil fuels originate from trees and plants, which naturally hold large amounts of carbon dioxide. Once this carbon dioxide (along with other gases) is in Earth's atmosphere, it traps heat and causes Earth's temperature to slowly rise. This will affect future generations in several ways, including changes in climate and a rise in sea levels.

What you can do to help sustainability

Try to make sure that you use sustainable **resources**.
Ride a bicycle or walk instead of driving.
Eat locally grown food.

The Roadless Area Conservation Rule

In 2004, the U.S. government announced plans to repeal (cancel) the Roadless Area Conservation Rule. The Rule stopped people from building roads in wild forest areas. Without roads it was impossible for logging companies to chop down trees in the forests, since there was no way of getting the cutters in or the timber out. The Rule therefore protected forests from logging.

The plans to repeal the Rule would affect about 58.5 million acres of forest that could then be opened to logging. These forests help provide clean water for people, homes for wild animals and plants, and streams and lakes for fishing. Many of the old trees that make up these forests would provide very valuable lumber, but it would take many years to grow replacements once they have been cut down. Protesters argue that cutting down the forests would badly affect the lives of future generations of Americans.

The price of profit

Human greed affects our ability to live in a sustainable way. The desire to make larger and larger profits has a big impact on our environment. Loggers want to access the forests of the United States so they can make money from the timber that grows there. Cod stocks have been almost **fished out** because fishers ignored the signs that they were taking too many from the sea. Around the world, fishers preferred to make money from larger catches, rather than take smaller catches, but preserve fish stocks. The loggers and fishers argue—correctly—that people want to buy what they are selling.

People's everyday individual choices also affect sustainability. Choices such as which fish to eat for dinner or which lumber to buy for a new garden fence have long-term effects on the world. We are all responsible, not just those businesses that directly take resources from the environment.

What you can do

Contact the Forestry Stewardship Council to find out ways of identifying sustainably harvested wood.

Hundreds of truckloads of trees are cut down from the world's forests each day. Very few are replaced by new trees.

Cod

Cod has been a popular food for thousands of years. Popular cod dishes include fish and chips in England, chowder in North America, and salt cod in Spain, Portugal, West Africa, and the Caribbean. There is even evidence that Basque cod fishers reached North America years before Columbus—but kept it secret, because they did not want rival fishers to know about the rich cod-fishing areas off the coast.

Today, these same Atlantic cod-fishing areas are in trouble. Ships have been hauling in nets full of fish for centuries. The average size of fish being caught has gotten smaller and smaller. This is because fish are being caught before they have had a chance to grow to a large size. The fishers were concerned with making as much money as possible. No one was making sure there were enough cod left to breed more fish for the future. Fishing has had to be stopped in some areas because so many fish have now been taken.

Some scientists believe closing the fisheries may not even solve the problem. Other types of fish have moved into the cod's territory and are eating the food cod once fed on. Cod may have lost its place in the **food chain**. If so, its numbers might never recover.

The cod being caught now are, on average, younger fish than the cod caught in previous decades.

The demand for resources

Increases in population have put more strain on the world's resources. Some resources are practically infinite. If we could take all our energy from solar power, for example, there would be energy as long as the sun kept rising in the morning. Other resources are finite, meaning that once they run out they cannot be replaced. Fossil fuels such as oil are examples of a finite resource.

Even our most basic resources are coming under increasing pressure. For example, many people in richer countries take water for granted. Open a tap or turn on a shower, and water is readily available. But by 2025, two-thirds of the world's population is likely to be short of water.

WATER DEMAND

Some of the parts of the world where water is in shortest supply—such as parts of sub-Saharan Africa—are areas with rising populations. Everyone needs water to survive, so experts predict that battles over water resources will become a cause of conflict in years to come. Already, commercial companies are buying exclusive rights to some rivers and aquifers. They plan to profit from the water these contain, and their profits will rise as the water level sinks lower. But only those who can pay will have access to the water.

Rising population is not the only problem affecting our water resources. Overall, each person is using an increasing amount of water. As parts of the world become richer, people's habits change. People that once washed using a cloth and a bowl of water now take showers or baths. People that once washed the dishes themselves now have dishwashers. Taking a shower or using a dishwasher uses more than 9 gallons (34 liters) of water; taking a bath uses up to 20 gallons (76 liters). Using a bowl to wash uses just 1 gallon (3.8 liters). Each time you flush the toilet, it uses around 2.6 gallons (9.8 liters) of water. As the number of people who have toilets increases, more water will be flushed away.

Egypt's civilization grew up around its chief water supply, the River Nile. Traditional boats called dhows still carry people and produce up and down the river.

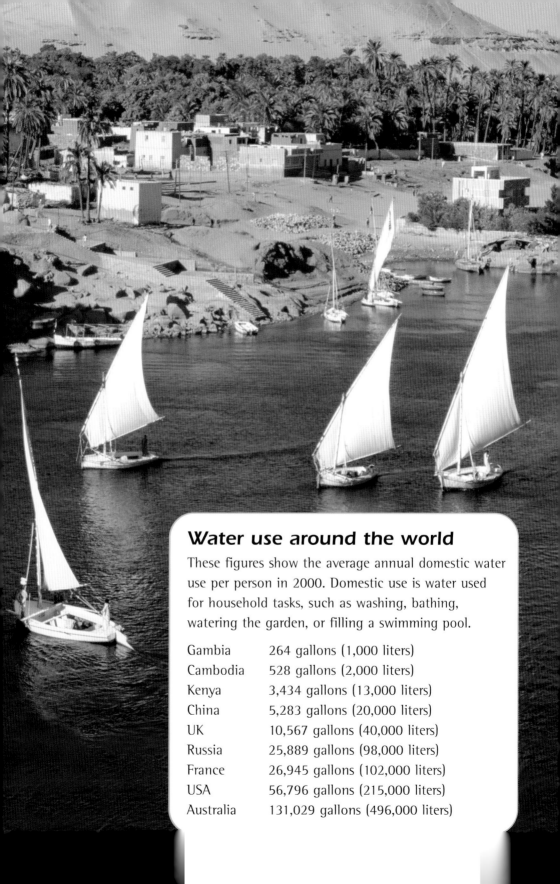

Water use around the world

These figures show the average annual domestic water use per person in 2000. Domestic use is water used for household tasks, such as washing, bathing, watering the garden, or filling a swimming pool.

Gambia	264 gallons (1,000 liters)
Cambodia	528 gallons (2,000 liters)
Kenya	3,434 gallons (13,000 liters)
China	5,283 gallons (20,000 liters)
UK	10,567 gallons (40,000 liters)
Russia	25,889 gallons (98,000 liters)
France	26,945 gallons (102,000 liters)
USA	56,796 gallons (215,000 liters)
Australia	131,029 gallons (496,000 liters)

The cost of affluence

The term affluence refers to wealth, especially when that wealth is used to buy many material goods. What seems affluent differs from place to place. In central India, a man who can afford a motorcycle and who owns five cows might seem affluent to his neighbors. In Sydney, Australia, owning a home in the city and another near the beach, having two cars, and eating in restaurants most evenings might make someone appear affluent.

CHANGING EXPECTATIONS

Around the world, people's expectations for their own lives are changing. Television and the Internet have spread new ideas of what makes life good. Often these ideas are based on things seen in wealthy countries—things like expensive cars, fancy clothes, and other **consumer goods**. This has created an increased demand for the world's resources, which are used to make these goods and to keep them running. One good example of this is the world's increased desire for cars.

GLOBAL TRAFFIC JAM

Cars have various benefits for people. People with cars can move around easily while carrying goods, children, or friends with them. Many car owners cannot imagine how they could cope without their vehicles. But gasoline-powered cars are manufactured with finite resources such as metals, and these vehicles burn gasoline and create pollution as they run.

*As car use has increased, so too have deaths on the world's roads. An estimated 3,000 people die in car accidents each day—more than are killed by **malaria**.*

Car ownership and use has greatly increased since World War II. In fact, the car population has grown five times as fast as the human population. The countries with the highest numbers of cars are the world's richest countries. Canada, the United States, Italy, Japan, Australia, and New Zealand are among the places where there are more than 500 cars for every 1,000 people. At the other extreme, India and China were reported to have 10 cars or fewer for every 1,000 people in the year 2000.

At the moment, the countries with the highest populations have the lowest levels of car ownership. However, the rate of car ownership is increasing fastest in countries like China. In 2004, a mini-crisis in the price of oil was partly sparked by China's increased need for oil. This was not only oil for vehicles—it was also for use in industry. But even this industrial use was created by the world's increasing demand for consumer goods, many of them manufactured in China.

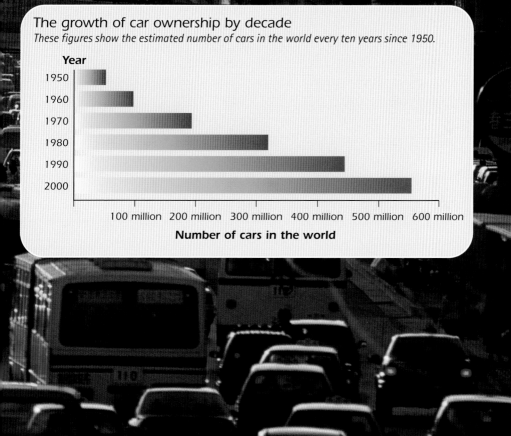

The growth of car ownership by decade
These figures show the estimated number of cars in the world every ten years since 1950.

Year

| 1950 |
| 1960 |
| 1970 |
| 1980 |
| 1990 |
| 2000 |

100 million   200 million   300 million   400 million   500 million   600 million

Number of cars in the world

An aging population

In some of the world's wealthy countries, the changing **demographics** can cause significant problems. In many wealthy countries, people are living longer due to improved health care. They are also having fewer children. The population stays at about the same size, but there are not as many babies and young people, and there are more old people. The population chart begins to look like a mushroom rather than a pyramid (see pages 10 and 11).

In some wealthy countries, the population is increasing by less than one percent a year, and the aging population could create trouble for the future. Citizens in some countries are used to a high standard of health care and expect to get social security benefits when they retire. These benefits are provided from **taxes** paid by people who are working. But if there are more old people and less young workers, there may not be enough money coming in as taxes to pay for good healthcare and social security.

Older people are living longer and more active lives than ever before, meaning many populations are "graying" or getting older.

Providers and dependents

This graphic shows how many **dependents** (people in the over-64 or under-15 categories) there were in different parts of the world in 2001. These dependents probably had to be supported by those in the working population (the 15-to-64 category).

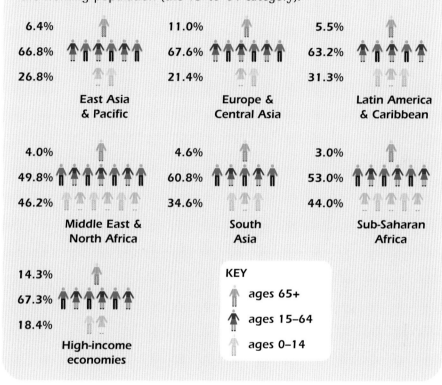

	East Asia & Pacific	Europe & Central Asia	Latin America & Caribbean
	6.4%	11.0%	5.5%
	66.8%	67.6%	63.2%
	26.8%	21.4%	31.3%

	Middle East & North Africa	South Asia	Sub-Saharan Africa
	4.0%	4.6%	3.0%
	49.8%	60.8%	53.0%
	46.2%	34.6%	44.0%

High-income economies
14.3%
67.3%
18.4%

KEY

ages 65+

ages 15–64

ages 0–14

FUTURE IMPACTS

In the future, countries may offer private retirement plans instead of federal or state plans. In private plans, the size of people's benefits depends on how much they paid into them while they were working. People who have been poor all their lives will remain poor after they have retired. Healthcare will probably be provided on a similar basis.

The alternative to private retirement plans and healthcare would be for working people to pay increasingly larger amounts of tax. Some countries take high taxes from their citizens so that even those people with small incomes can have a good lifestyle. However, this is unlikely to be popular in countries where wealthy people are not used to paying high taxes.

Debates About Population

Global v. personal

There are many practical reasons why governments find it difficult to control population growth. For example, sometimes people feel they need to have many children who can eventually help earn money for the family; in other cases they do not have access to **contraception**. Another reason is that people may feel that it is their right to have children and that governments should not intervene. In some countries large families are traditional.

Population figures are collected on regional, national, and global bases, but each child added to the world's population is a matter of individual choice. This poses a problem for governments that want to limit the growth of their populations, especially in **democratic** societies. Such limits on the size of the population tend to be unpopular, as the majority of people either already have, or plan to have, children at some time. In wealthy countries, the birth rate is already low (see pages 15 and 20–21), so this is less of a problem. But in poorer countries, where populations are rising rapidly, governments must tread very carefully in their attempts to limit the number of children people have.

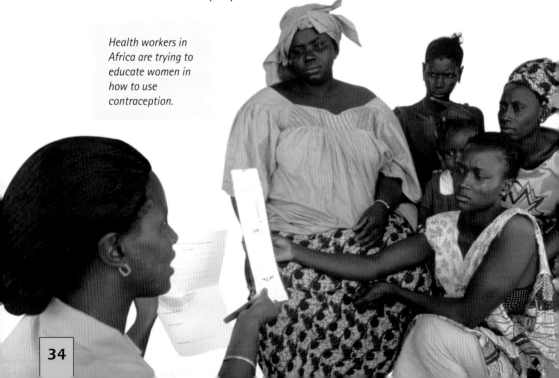

Health workers in Africa are trying to educate women in how to use contraception.

Affecting individual choice

Governments try to influence people's decisions to have children in several ways, including the following:

EDUCATION

Education plays a role in persuading people to have fewer children. There is a link between literacy rates and birth rates in poor countries. As the literacy rate rises, the birth rate goes down. Governments can also run ad campaigns—using radio, TV, and newspaper—to persuade people to have fewer children.

GOVERNMENT AID

Encouragement for people to have children often takes the form of government help for people with children. In the United States, for example, parents can get tax credits and other assistance for having children. Most of the world's wealthy countries offer free schooling for all children.

In some developed countries employers are required to provide child-care for employees with young children.

35

COSTS AND CHILDREN

Governments sometimes try to discourage people from having children by making it more expensive. This might be done by withdrawing help for people with children, or increasing taxes on things parents need. In extreme cases, such as in China (see case study opposite), the government can fine people who have more children than they are allowed.

Controlling birth rates has generally been most successful in Asia, especially in countries with un-democratic governments where people cannot vote against population control.

This photo shows a statue of the Chinese Communist ruler Mao Zedong leading his people. The Communist regime in China, under the rule of Mao, imposed limits on the number of children couples could have.

China's one-child policy

Under the leadership of the **communist** ruler Mao Zedong, China's population began to grow rapidly in the years following World War II. China's leaders became concerned that the population was getting so big that it would surpass China's ability to feed itself. In 1979 they began the "one child policy." This ruled that no family was supposed to have more than one child. If they did, they were fined by the state.

The policy is not always strictly enforced. In rural areas, for example, people ignore it and have more children so that they can help work the land. There are other exceptions. China's **ethnic minorities** are not included in the one-child policy, though there are rumors that they have sometimes been forced to join it. If neither parent has brothers or sisters they are allowed to have more than one child. However, the children must be at least four years apart in age. A family whose child has disabilities is also sometimes allowed a second child.

Recently there have been suggestions that China would like to relax the one-child policy because it has been too successful. In 2003, Shanghai had 57,000 births and 100,700 deaths, with the population declining at a rate of 3.24 people per 1000. 2003 was the eleventh year in a row that the city's population had fallen, and the Commission of Population and Birth Control there is now says that this is "unhealthy."

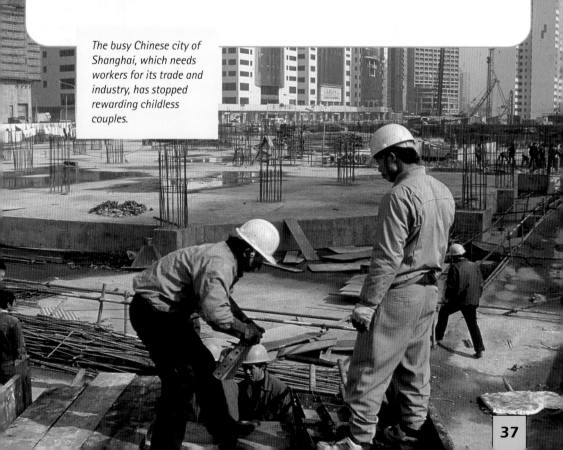

The busy Chinese city of Shanghai, which needs workers for its trade and industry, has stopped rewarding childless couples.

Teenage pregnancy

Many countries have made efforts to control the birth rate among teenage mothers. Teenage mothers often suffer from poverty. They may not have finished their own education and this, combined with having to care for a small child, can mean they find life financially very difficult.

The highest rates of teenage pregnancy are in the world's poorest countries. In sub-Saharan Africa, for example, 138 of every 1,000 babies born in 2002 were born to women between 15 and 19 years old. Compare this to the world's richest countries, where the figure averaged just 24 per 1,000.

OBJECTIONS TO POPULATION CONTROL

Not everyone thinks that controlling the size of the world's population is a good idea. There are many religions and other groups who believe we should not try to control the number of children people have. They may take the view that it is up to God, not humans, whether people conceive a child.

Record numbers of young children in the developing world mean that populations will increase for decades to come. This is because large numbers of young people today will be the parents of future generations.

THE POSSIBILITY OF ADOPTION

Religious and other groups sometimes argue that it would be better for babies to be adopted than for people to use contraception to avoid having children. They argue that many people want to adopt a child and would be able to give it a good home and a happy life.

In wealthy countries, many women decide to delay having children until they are older. This can make it difficult or impossible to conceive, and partly for this reason there is a long waiting list of people hoping to adopt a baby. Some people have adopted a baby from another, poorer part of the world, hoping to give the baby a better life. Critics point out that they also avoid the selection procedures and waiting lists at home. Many governments are now acting to make it harder to adopt children from abroad.

Falling birth rates

Birth rates in many poorer regions of the world fell over the 21 years between 1980 and 2001. However, they are still at a rate that means the population is growing.

Region	1980 birth rate per woman	2001 birth rate per woman
Sub-Saharan Africa	6.6	5.1
Middle East and North Africa	6.2	3.3
South Asia	5.3	3.2

Future Populations

The growth in the world's population is set to place an increasing strain on the world's resources. As the numbers and expectations of the world's people increase, these people demand more living space, water, food, and other resources. The United Nations predicts that by 2050, the world's population will be nine billion people.

In some parts of the world, governments already find it impossible to make sure all their people have enough food, drink, good homes, healthcare, and education. If the world's population increases by another 50 percent, this will become even more difficult. Many experts predict that the wars of the 21st century could be fought over the world's shrinking resources.

The elephant in the hallway

Imagine a family that has an elephant living in the hallway of their house. Yet they do not acknowledge that the elephant is there. Instead, they step around the elephant and pretend there is nothing in the way. In some ways, we are like the family, and the world's population is our elephant. It is sitting in the hallway, growing bigger every year, and we just keep trying to squeeze around it.

We can see the problems coming, but do not seem to be dealing with them. So what could we do?

- *Use fewer resources*. If everyone used fewer resources—less gasoline, water, energy, and consumer goods—they would last longer.

- *Make what we have go further*. Science and technology may help us make our resources last longer. Some cars, for example, can now run on a combination of gasoline and electricity, meaning they use far less gasoline.

- *Find alternatives*. Using renewable energy, or bicycles instead of cars, could mean that some resources would no longer be so crucial.

- *Control population growth*. Making efforts to slow down or stop the world's population growth would help to reduce the pressure on resources.

Hope for the future?

There is hope for the future. To some extent, population growth is related to increasing wealth, which brings better healthcare and **sanitation**. As people's wealth increases still further, they tend to have fewer children, until—as in many wealthy countries today—the population starts to fall. Some demographers are now predicting that by the late 21st century, the world's overall population will have started to decline.

Statistical Information

WORLD POPULATION, PAST AND PREDICTED

Year (c.e.)	Number of people
1	300,000,000
1000	310,000,000
1900	1,650,000,000
2000	6,000,000,000
2015	7,100,000,000
2025	7,700,000,000
2050	9,000,000,000

*The **United Nations** estimates that between 2001 and 2025, more than 1.6 billion people will be added to the world's population, 96 percent of them in low- to middle-income economies.*

MOST POPULOUS COUNTRIES

1 China*	1,278,900,000
2 India	1,032,400,000
3 United States	285,300,000
4 Indonesia	209,000,000
5 Brazil	172,400,000
6 Russian Federation	144,800,000
7 Nigeria	129,900,000

*includes Hong Kong and Macao

In 2001 China still led the list of countries with the largest populations, despite its one-child policy.

GROWTH RATES

Population growth is predicted to slow over the coming decades. World population growth stood at 1.4 percent in the years 1990 to 2001. From 2001 to 2015 it is predicted to fall to 1.0 percent ; from 2015 to 2025, the rate is expected to fall to 0.8 percent.

Region	2001	2015	2025
East Asia/Pacific	1,823	+220	+134
Europe/Central Asia	476	+ 1	+ 2
Latin America/Caribbean	519	+107	+ 68
Middle East/North Africa	300	+ 89	+ 59
South Asia	1,378	+302	+189
Sub-Saharan Africa	673	+207	+156

This table shows the 2001 populations of selected parts of the world, and then their predicted population increases by 2015 and by 2025. All figures are in millions.

LIFE EXPECTANCY

Life expectancy has risen in all parts of the world except sub-Saharan Africa.

- The fall in life expectancy in sub-Saharan Africa is largely due to the AIDS epidemic and the continent's civil wars. For example, between 1990 and 2001, life expectancy fell by 18 years in Botswana.
- In Europe overall, life expectancy has been affected by changes in countries that were once part of the USSR. In the Russian Federation, for example, life expectancy fell by 3 years between 1990 and 2001.

Region	1980 life expectancy	2001 life expectancy
East Asia/Pacific	64	69
Europe/Central Asia	68	69
Latin America/Caribbean	65	71
Middle East/North Africa	58	68
South Asia	54	63
Sub-Saharan Africa	48	46

In 2001 life expectancy was below 40 years in the following countries:

- Sierra Leone
- Botswana
- Zimbabwe
- Zambia
- Malawi.

All except one of the countries with a life expectancy of below 50 were also in sub-Saharan Africa; the exception was Afghanistan.

FAMILY SIZE

Around the world, family sizes are falling.

- Birth rates in Western and Central Europe, Canada, China, Japan, Thailand, and Australia are all below 2 births per woman.
- In South America, Mexico, the United States, North Africa, India, Indonesia, southern Africa, and the Russian Federation, rates are between 2 and 3.9 births per woman.
- In sub-Saharan Africa, much of the Middle East, Pakistan, Afghanistan, Haiti, Guatemala, and El Salvador, rates are between 4 and 7 births per woman.

GLOSSARY

aquifer underground layer of rock or sand that holds water

carbon dioxide gas produced when carbon fuels are burned

cholera fatal disease that causes vomiting and diarrhea

civil war war between groups who live in the same country

communist person who believes that businesses, farms, and other concerns should be owned by the state or people, instead of wealthy individuals

consumer goods items manufactured for sale to ordinary people, such as cars, TVs, washing machines, and refrigerators

contraception method of preventing a woman from becoming pregnant

deforested area of forest where all or most of the trees have been cut down

democratic society in which everyone has a choice in deciding how their country is run

demographer person who studies human populations, including their size and distribution

demographics characteristics of a human population, including its size, growth, age, density, distribution, and statistics regarding birth, marriage, disease, and death

dependent person who relies on someone else to care for them. For example, young children are dependent on their parents.

emigration act of leaving one country or region to live in another

environment surroundings

ethnic minority group of people who share a background and culture, such as stories, songs, and the place they originally came from

fished out without enough fish to catch

food chain group of plants and/or animals that depend on eating one another for survival

fragmentation the breaking of something into small pieces

immigration people moving into a new country to live

infant mortality death of a child before it reaches one year old

inheritance goods or money left behind when someone dies

irrigation water used to help crops grow

life expectancy average lifespan

literacy ability to read

malaria disease that causes chills and fever, and sometimes death

nutrients things that sustain life, such as the minerals in soil that help plants grow, or the parts of food such as fats, carbohydrates, and proteins that support human life

only child child without any brothers or sisters

pension payment made to a person by governments or companies after he or she has stopped working

persecution cruel or unfair treatment. Many migrants and refugees leave their homes in an attempt to escape persecution.

rainforest thick, dense forest with a lot of rain all year round

resources supply of materials

retiring stopping work through choice, often because of age. In many countries there is a set age when people are expected to retire.

sanitation the provision of clean water and sewage systems to prevent disease

subsistence agriculture type of farming in which a farmer grows only enough for his or her family to eat

summit a conference of high-level leaders, usually called to make a plan of action

taxes payments demanded by the government. Taxes are usually a percentage of a sum of money. Income tax, for example, could be twenty percent of each person's income.

tsunami giant wave usually caused by an earthquake on the sea bed

tuberculosis disease of the lungs that often kills people unless it is treated

United Nations global organization of most of the world's governments. It tries to work together to solve some of the world's problems.

Further Reading

Books

Gifford, Clive. *Refugees*. London: Chrysalis Children's Books, 2002.
This title examines some the reasons why people are forced to flee to new countries, as well as the kinds of welcome they may receive when they get there.

Millstone, Erik and Lang, Tim. *The Atlas of Food: Who Eats What, Where, and Why*. New York: Penguin, 2003.
A sister publication to *The State of the World Atlas* (see below), this useful book provides information on almost every aspect of food and the health issues associated with it, including the ways in which population and food are interrelated.

Smith, Dan. *The State of the World Atlas*. New York: Penguin, 2003.
This book offers an invaluable, map-based graphic presentation of facts and figures under such headings as Power, Cost of Living, Rights, and Life and Death. The book provides comparisons between different parts of the world, interesting statistics, and text explaining the facts in short passages. This book is regularly reprinted and updated.

The World Bank. *Mini Atlas of Global Development*. The World Bank, 2004.
Under the headings People, Health, Economy, Environment, and Global Links, this pocket-sized book contains a world of information. Do you want to know how many people in China have personal computers, or in which countries less than half of the population can read? You'll find out here

Websites

Center for Public Information on Population Research
www.prb.org/cpipr
This group attempts to explain the meaning of current pieces of research into population and population trends.

Department For International Development (DFID)
www.dfid.gov.uk
The UK Government's website for the Department For International Development (DFID) has lots of useful information about population issues.

Oxfam International
www.oxfam.org
Oxfam is one of the oldest organizations campaigning and working against poverty in the world's poorest countries. Follow the links to visit their country sites around the world, where you can find out about the issues facing families there.

Population Reference Bureau
www.prb.org
This website provides up-to-date information on population trends in almost all the world's countries.

United Nations Schools Site
www.un.org/cyberschoolbus
Learn about population and the work of the United Nations.

United States Agency for International Development (USAID)
www.usaid.gov
USAID is the United State's main provider of aid and poverty assistance overseas.

INDEX